JOHN PHILOPONUS
THEOLOGIAN, ASTRONOMER, PHILOSPHER

JOHN PHILOPONUS
THEOLOGIAN, ASTRONOMER, PHILOSPHER

Translated by Fr Robert Nixon, OSB

Introduced by Fr John St Shenouda

ST SHENOUDA PRESS
SYDNEY, AUSTRALIA
2024

JOHN PHILOPONUS,
Theologian, Astronomer, Philospher

Translated By: Fr Robert Nixon
Introduced By: Fr John St. Shenouda

COPYRIGHT © 2024
St. Shenouda Press

All rights reserved. Except for brief quotations in critical publications or reviews, no part of this book may be reproduced in any manner without prior written permission from the publisher.

ST SHENOUDA PRESS
8419 Putty Rd,
Putty, NSW, 2330
Sydney, Australia

www.stshenoudapress.com

ISBN 13: 978-1-7635450-1-4

All scripture quotations, unless otherwise indicated, are taken from the New King James Version®. Copyright © 1982 by Thomas Nelson, Inc. Used by permission. All rights reserved.

Cover Design:
Dionysia Tanios
@dionysiandesigns

Contents

Introduction	7
The Arbiter or The Wise Judge A philosophical demonstration of the unity of Christ	21
Translator's Note	23
Prologue	27
Chapter I	35
Chapter II	41
Chapter III	43
Chapter IV	47
Chapter V	51
Chapter VI	53
Chapter VII	55
Chapter VIII	61
Chapter IX	64
Chapter X	65
Epilogue	76
Introduction Bibliography	77

Introduction

John Philoponus, also known as John the Grammarian or John of Alexandria, was a Christian philosopher, theologian, scientist, and literary scholar. 'Philoponus' literally means 'lover of toil/work'[6]. Philoponus was born in Alexandria around 490 A.D., was converted to Christianity in about 520 A.D., and lived approximately until 570 A.D. He is the author of numerous philosophical treatises and theological works. Although Philoponus initially started as a proponent and defender of Aristotle, later his originality through his writings and methodology broke free from the Aristotelian-Neoplatonic tradition of his time, which led to a more explanatory and empirical approach to the natural world of science. Among Philoponus' numerous contributions and achievements, probably most significant is the contribution he initiated which eventually resulted in the demise of Aristotelianism, or Aristotelian philosophy. Also of note are his scientific contributions that made an impact at the time and also modern day, and both Syriac and Arabic cultures, and medieval Western thought. Although Philoponus was condemned both during his era and after his death, in recent years modern day scholarship has done quite a lot to really start to appreciate and value his works and accomplishments of this 'original' thinker and important philosopher. The influence of Philoponus has certainly been enhanced due to the fact that his treatises have become more widely studied and translated.

The works of Philoponus consist of at least 40 treatises on a range of topics such as theology, mathematics, sciences (cosmology, physics, astronomy), church politics and even medical treatises.

[6] Konstantinos Kalachanis Prof. Efstratios Theodossiou Evangelia Panou Vassilios Manimanisloannis Kostikas, The Perception of Time by Humans according to John Philoponus and its relation with the Theory of Special and General Relativity, Internation Journal of Humanities and Social Science Vol. 3 No. 20; December 2013, 279

Unfortunately, not all of his works are extant and some are fragmentary, being known indirectly through quotations rather than complete treatises.

Very little is known of the early life of Philoponus. He was a native of Alexandria, Egypt, and studied at the school of Alexandria. He was a student of the well-known Aristotelian philosopher Ammonius, the son of Hermias. Shortly after, Philoponus began to develop his own ideas and views evident in his writings which he probably began publishing from about 510 A.D. One of his own ideas, although at the time it was effectively unrecognised and largely ignored, was when Philoponus helped develop the 'pre-cursor' concept of inertia which was famously developed and attributed to Galileo and Isaac Newton many centuries later. This was proposed in what was called the 'theory of impetus', which stated that "an object moves and continues to move because of an energy imparted in it by the mover and ceases the movement when that energy is exhausted"[7]. This concept was revolutionary and stirred the pot, one could say, and it helps to explain this proposal in context of the time period that he lived.

At the time Aristotle initially stated the principle of inertia relatively correctly:

"No one could say why something that is moving should stop anywhere; why should it stop here rather than there? Therefore, a thing will either be at rest or must move forever, unless something more powerful get in its way."[8]

However, Aristotle then believed and asserted that air was needed as a force to keep an object moving, such as a rock being thrown. Philoponus subsequently challenged this argument, on the basis of experience and experiment, in his book On Aristotle Physics using the example of placing projectiles on a wall rather

---

7 T. Kelly, The A to Z of People of Faith and Science: Short Biographies (ATF Press, 2018). https://books.google.com.au/books?id=Le-YDwAAQBAJ. 20
8 J.D. Current, Physics Related to Anesthesia (PediaPress GmbH, 2010). https://books.google.com.au/books?id=RgcpOQ444vgC.

than being launched, which may move but only as far enough to fall from the wall.⁹ One could argue that just Philoponus developing this foreshadowing concept of inertia ranks him among the great scientific minds of his time and also all history. This principle of Philoponus, and he developed other scientific models, emphasises that this work was one of the fundamental precursors to modern physics and science.

Philoponus also directly opposed Aristotle's view that "the speed at which two identically shaped objects sink or fall is directly proportional to their weights and inversely proportional to the density of the medium through which they move"¹⁰. This opposition further cemented Philoponus' place as going against the norm, but perhaps one could say all for the greater good. This proposal was made more than a thousand years before Galileo, in another kind of pre-cursor to modern day physics. Philoponus was able to come to this proposal by reviewing the claims made by Aristotle with an experiment dropping different sized weights. He concluded, in direct contrary to Aristotle once again, that heavier weights did not fall much faster than lighter ones, disclaiming Aristotle's claim of inverse proportionality.

We can quote Philoponus to help explain some light on this 'original' contribution and opposition to Aristotle:

"But this [view of Aristotle] is completely erroneous, and our view may be completely corroborated by actual observation more effectively than by any sort of verbal argument.¹¹

For if you let fall from the same height two weights, one many times heavier than the other you will see that the ratio of the

---

9 R. Sorabji, Philoponus and the Rejection of Aristotelian Science (Institute of Classical Studies, School of Advanced Study, University of London, 2010). https://books.google.com.au/books?id=EW5CAQAAIAAJ. 129
10 Gindikin, S.G. (1988). Tales of Physicists and Mathematicians. Birkh, 29 9
11 P. Lang, Science: Antiquity and its Legacy (Bloomsbury Publishing, 2015). https://books.google.com.au/books?id=dbeKDwAAQBAJ. 65

times required for the motion does not depend [solely] on the weights, but that the difference in time is very small."[12]

In contrast though, one must not overstate Philoponus' positive account of velocity for two reasons. First, he believes, incorrectly, that their will be a marginal difference in falling speed according to the weight of the body[13]. He concurred with Aristotle thinking that velocity increases with heaviness by stating, "the more heavy bodies are combined, the greater will be the speed at which they move"[14]. Philoponus also says, "the same space will consequently be traversed by the heavier body in a shorter time and by the lighter body in a longer time"[15]. Secondly, though we do not want to get too technical, we are just trying to make a point of objective criticism, was that Philoponus referred to gross weight rather than specific weight[16]. However, we don't want to take anything away from the tremendous contribution of Philoponus here. Without question, this particular work of Philoponus was breaking new ground and foreshadowed the work of Galileo when he gathered further evidence to conclude that objects fall at the same rate irrespective of their masses.

In 529 A.D. Philoponus wrote the treatise On the eternity of the world against Proclus, which is quite a significant work. This critical work is basically a full-frontal systematic attack on the argument put forward by Proclus that the world is eternal, and argues rather that the world had a beginning and was even "mandatory of the pagan own principles"[17]. The importance of this work cannot be underestimated as he proposed the initial

---

12 Morris R. Cohen and I. E. Drabkin (eds 1958), A Source Book in Greek Science, 220
13 Sorabji, Philoponus and the Rejection of Aristotelian Science. 54
14 (in Phys 683, 16-25
15 In phys 679, 20-21
16 "The specific weight takes into account the volume of a body and permits a direct mathematical comparison between the falling body and the medium through which it falls" Sorabji, Philoponus and the Rejection of Aristotelian Science. 54
17 Ventureyra, Scott. "John Philoponus Contra Aristotle: The Emergence of Consciousness in Light of Contemporary Cosmology and Philosophy." Science Et Esprit, 2020. 138

Introduction

Kalam Cosmological argument which has been supported through modern scientific evidence – via both the expansion of the universe and the second law of thermodynamics. Philoponus, about 1500 years ago, proposed a deductive argument for the existence of God;

1. Whatever comes to be has a cause of its coming to be.

2. The universe came to be

3. Therefore, the universe has a cause of its coming to be.

Recently this argument has been revived in light of the many centuries where the main belief was the worldview that the earth was eternal. While Philoponus was likely influenced by his predecessors such as Athanasius the Apostolic, Basil of Caesarea and Cyril of Alexandria, he was perhaps the "first Christian to take seriously for the physics of the world the Christian doctrines of 'Creation out of nothing' and 'The Incarnation' in its space and time"[18]. This argument on its own had an influence and indebt to Philoponus by many philosophers and theologians, probably too numerous to mention.

Philoponus was very intelligent and used his deep knowledge of the Neoplatonist and Aristotelian beliefs to counter the views of Paganism against themselves[19]. He was critical of Aristotle's concept of infinity and used it as refutation to nuance his argument that the world was not eternal. He said, "the universe had a beginning, because otherwise it would have gone right through an actual infinity, a more than finite number, of years"[20]. We may currently accept that in a manner "the set of whole

---

[18] Thomas Torrance's mission to Lift J. Philoponus' Anathemas, with George Dragas and John McKenna support after Richard Sorabji's enthusiastic research to rescue the Alexandrian Polymath from Oblivion!, 5

[19] Sorabji, Philoponus and the Rejection of Aristotelian Science. 208

[20] J. Philoponus and M.J. Share, Against Proclus on the Eternity of the World 1-5 (Duckworth, 2004). https://books.google.com.au/books?id=iuvWAAAAMAAJ. preface viii

numbers has more members than the set of odd numbers, but then such an idea was widely considered absurd"[21].

Some more quotes from Philoponus in his work against Proclus on the eternity of the world are outlined here in attempt to explain and simplify;

"And if anyone insists on maintaining that the infinite should not be held responsible for more things not having been created, but simply says that it is not only an infinite number of things that cannot have come to be but not even any more at all than exist…how could it be other than absurd to claim than God could not bring natural animals of this kind into existence?[22]

"So, just as we conceive of non-being not as a kind of existence, but only as privation of being, so too are we persuaded that shadow is merely privation of light and not a kind of existence imbued with form that is created by bodies. So how could one take the passing out of existence of light that arises from the interposition of bodies as a parallel to the generation and existence of the world which stem from God?" [23]

Also, "For if, as the cone of shadow moves round, it spreads over different parts of the moon's sphere in turn and prevents the sun's light from reaching them it is clear that light diffused there too is not, as Proclus claims, imperishable but perishable" [24]. Philoponus undertook to demonstrate the creation of the world by showing that the assumption of eternal motion has impossible implication[25]. He argued that the world is a corporeal object

---

21 J. Zachhuber, The Rise of Christian Theology and the End of Ancient Metaphysics: Patristic Philosophy from the Cappadocian Fathers to John of Damascus (Oxford University Press, 2020). https://books.google.com.au/books?id=PnbnD-wAAQBAJ. 24
22 Philoponus and Share, Against Proclus on the Eternity of the World 1-5. 25
23 Philoponus and Share, Against Proclus on the Eternity of the World 1-5. 27
24 Philoponus and Share, Against Proclus on the Eternity of the World 1-5. 29
25 Herbert A. Davidson, "John Philoponus as a Source of Medieval Islamic and Jewish Proofs of Creation," Journal of the American Oriental Society 89, no. 2 (1969), https://doi.org/10.2307/596519, http://www.jstor.org/stable/596519. 358

Introduction

Apostolic, contains only finite power, and therefore could not have existed from all eternity but must be generated[26].

The work of Philoponus 'on the eternity of the world against Proclus' is interesting in the sense that Philoponus effectively disclaims literally every argument and point made by Proclus. It is also interesting that despite Philoponus being certainly a Christian, and this work is at least in part motivated and derived from his Christian faith which clearly ascribes to the Christian worldview of having a beginning, he seems to have intentionally kept biblical theology out of this polemic and combated Proclus solely using the framework of Greek philosophy.[27] The Greek philosophers taught in their schools the rejection of the concept that creation come out of nothing and this never occurs in nature, which Philoponus used to his advantage.

It is probably fair to say that unfortunately, the style of Philoponus' commentaries and his 'controversial' conclusions resulted in him being unpopular among his contemporary philosophers. His methods and efforts to unite reason and experience in the time of Aristotle was another type or order, and perhaps this 'rocking of the boat' so to speak led to him being utterly condemned and eventually anathematized. Maybe for this reason in the later part of his life he focused and devoted himself to almost exclusively theological writings, with his last philosophical work attributed around 530 A.D. For example, in 550 A.D. Philoponus wrote the theological work On the Creation of the World. Also, Philoponus wrote The Arbiter in approximately 552 A.D, one of his most important and widespread theological works post-Chalcedonian, where he attempted, as much as possible, to be a non-biased arbiter/mediator between the miaphysite and Chalcedonian

---

26 Davidson, "John Philoponus as a Source of Medieval Islamic and Jewish Proofs of Creation." 13
27 Philoponus and Share, Against Proclus on the Eternity of the World 1-5.. 245, 22-246, 25

Christological models through mainly philosophical, rather than biblical, arguments[28].

As mentioned previously, the legacy of Philoponus was not only tarnished while he was alive, but seemed to be furthered stained even after his death. It's quite unfortunate that after about a century after Philoponus' death, the Church condemned him as a heretic claiming that he believed in the heretical doctrine that God was three separate persons in the trinity, as part of 'tritheism' belief.

Philoponus has not always got the credit he deserves, partly because of the Anathema which was imposed on him in A.D. 680, just over a hundred years after his death[29].

Other people assess Philoponus differently and view his thinking as far less characteristic as heresiological accounts would suggest[30]. It's important to note that from our Coptic Orthodox perspective, one can believe that Philoponus held miaphysite teaching, adhering to St. Cyril of Alexandria, who detailed at length the unity of Christ's humanity and divinity.[31] His application of Christology was founded in a miaphysite tradition, which the Byzantine church considered heresy.[32] While many will completely disagree with this claim, I believe that at least in part some of the controversy surrounding this

---

28 Benevich, Grigory. "John Philoponus and Maximus the Confessor at the Crossroads of Philosophical and Theological Thought in Late Antiquity." Scrinium. T. 7–8: Ars Christiana. In Memoriam Michail F. Murianov (21.XI.1928–6.VI.1995). Edited by R. Krivko, B. Lourié, and A. Orlov (Piscataway, NJ: Gorgias Press, 2011–2012) Part One. P. 102-13, 2012. 109

29 J.E. McKenna, The Setting in Life for The Arbiter of John Philoponos, 6th Century Alexandrian Scientist (Wipf and Stock Publishers, 1997). https://books.google.com.au/books?id=WWVKAwAAQBAJ. 31

30 A. Torrance and S. Paschalidis, Personhood in the Byzantine Christian Tradition: Early, Medieval, and Modern Perspectives (Taylor & Francis, 2018). https://books.google.com.au/books?id=oKVYDwAAQBAJ. 40.

31 Mateiescu, Sebastian, Philosophy, and Religious Studies. "John Philoponus and the Interpretation of Differentia in the Aftermath of Chalcedon." Aristotle in Byzantium (2020): 125–167. Print. 144

32 Zachhuber, The Rise of Christian Theology and the End of Ancient Metaphysics: Patristic Philosophy from the Cappadocian Fathers to John of Damascus. 3

alleged heresy was taken out of context. In further elaboration about this issue, perhaps a quote from Philoponus helps clarify his perspective and position:

We will neither, because Christ is one, deny the constituents of this 'one', nor, on the other hand, because we recognize two natures which have concurred into the union, will we not confess that 'one' which resulted from them; whether someone prefers to call it one nature or hypostasis or one Christ, makes no difference to us. For the rest will necessarily be implied by each of these[33]

Philoponus' definition of the 'one united nature' is not necessarily against his definition of the 'two natures'. Philoponos presumed that Cyril's confession that "there is one incarnate of God the word or Son" meant that there existed "one composite nature"[34]. In other words Christ is, after the union, a union of the 'two natures (divinity and humanity)' without confusing or changing them and without dividing or separating them. [35] This is stated in the Coptic Orthodox liturgy which says "He made It One with His divinity without mingling, without confusion, and without alteration".[36] Also in the midnight praises it says, "One nature out of two, divinity and humanity, therefore the Magi silently, worship uttering His divinity".[37] [38] . Thus it is argued

---

[33] U.M. Lang, John Philoponus and the Controversies Over Chalcedon in the Sixth Century: A Study and Translation of the Arbiter (Peeters, 2001). https://books.google.com.au/books?id=342CNwaH8vsC. 31

[34] John McKenna, The Concept of Nature in the Thought of John Philoponus And Other Essays (Grace Communion International, 2015). 9

[35] Thomas Torrance's mission to Lift J. Philoponus' Anathemas, with George Dragas and John McKenna support after Richard Sorabji's enthusiastic research to rescue the Alexandrian Polymath from Oblivion!, 15

[36] A. Botros and Saint George Coptic Orthodox Church, The Coptic Liturgy of Saint Basil with Raising of Incense (Saint George Coptic Orthodox Church, 1999). https://books.google.com.au/books?id=0YUbAAAACAAJ. 124

[37] Coptic Church, St. Bakhomious St. Mary, and St. Shenouda Coptic Orthodox Church, Midnight Praises (St Mary, St Bakhomios & St Shenouda Coptic Orthodox Church, 2007). https://books.google.com.au/books?id=fGVXNQAACAAJ. 78

[38] Thomas Torrance's mission to Lift J. Philoponus' Anathemas, with George Dragas and John McKenna support after Richard Sorabji's enthusiastic research to rescue the Alexandrian Polymath from Oblivion!, 22

that both Cyril's one united nature and Philoponus' one united nature intend to refer to the one and the same Christ and Son and Word of God, which Philoponus set out to attain through his argument in 'the Arbiter'[39]. It seems clear that Philoponus made some great and hard efforts to be coherent in the relationship between the three divine persons and the divine nature, and perhaps understandably there is confusion and disagreement of what he actually believed and conveyed. In any case, common ground seems to have been met by Philoponus by stating that there is one composite nature of Christ, united between divinity and humanity. Philoponus ultimately believed, arguably, that the end-product of Christ is one nature out of two.[40]

Philoponus caused additional controversy to his contemporaries after his work on the resurrection and in Against the letter of Dositheus by declaring in the resurrection that we (Christians) should receive new bodies rather than the old bodies.[41] By stating that the new body will be a different substance and nature it caused a bit of a storm because "Christians have always wanted to be sure that it would be we who were resurrected"[42]. Perhaps again this issue was taken out of context to further blow Philoponus' reputation, especially when he may well be arguing that after the resurrection there is a new type of matter that is superior to flesh, like Origen the scholar.[43] In addition, this work

---

39 Thomas Torrance's mission to Lift J. Philoponus' Anathemas, with George Dragas and John McKenna support after Richard Sorabji's enthusiastic research to rescue the Alexandrian Polymath from Oblivion!, 15

40 Lang, John Philoponus and the Controversies Over Chalcedon in the Sixth Century: A Study and Translation of the Arbiter. 57

41 5 Timotheus of Constantinople De receptione haereticorum PG 86, 44A; 61C; Nicephorus Callistus Ecclesiastica historia book 18, eh 47, PG 147, 424D; Paul of Antioch, in J.-B. Chabot, 'Documenta ad origines monophysitarum illustrandas', Corpus Scriptorum Christianorum Orientalium 17, Paris 1908, 330 (103, Louvain 1933, 230); John of Ephesus Historiae ecclesiasticae Part III Corpus Scriptorum Christianorum Orientalium 2.51, p 85,26-35; 3.17, p 106,12-16; cf 5.5, p 194,3 and 9, English translation by Payne Smit

42 Sorabji, Philoponus and the Rejection of Aristotelian Science. 73

43 Origen, On the Resurrection, found in The Biblical Repository, (Flagg & Gould, 1834). https://books.google.com.au/books?id=7oAXAAAAYAAJ. 665

Introduction

(among others) is extant only in fragments making it difficult to establish his argument(s) and definitively assess its breadth, coherence and overall significance. [44]

After Philoponus was excommunicated, this limited the spread of his work, particularly across the Byzantine empire, but in time his works have resurfaced in their circulation. Although some people, including religious figures, criticised the religious views of Philoponus, his scientific work was arguably quite flawless for his time and a foreshadowing of future scientific concepts and principles that are still studied today. Philoponus had an influence on many pagans, Christian, and even Muslim philosophers, theologians and scientists – including Galileo Galilei and Johannes Kepler just to name a few. In fact, Galileo mentioned Philoponus in his earlier writings more than even Plato, and inherited the impetus theory without directly mentioning Philoponus by name.[45] Ironically, demonstrating the extent of his Christian anathematisation, was that his first major initial impact was on the Islamic world rather than Christianity.[46] Philoponus planted intellectual seeds for future generations that really only seemed to 'catch' on and flower in the early 17th century when Galileo developed the framework models of Philoponus and enhanced the liberation from Aristotelian physics.

It is argued that, for Philoponus, there exists an actual articulation between both the science of his theology and the science of his philosophy. Philoponus did not confuse his theology upon his science or his science upon his theology but his theological comprehension of divine truth opened his eyes to a realistic understanding of the nature and its distinctive order to exert a regulative role in his choice and formation of scientific concepts and theories and their explanatory development.[47] However his

---

44 Zachhuber, The Rise of Christian Theology and the End of Ancient Metaphysics: Patristic Philosophy from the Cappadocian Fathers to John of Damascus. 4
45 Zachhuber, The Rise of Christian Theology and the End of Ancient Metaphysics: Patristic Philosophy from the Cappadocian Fathers to John of Damascus. ix
46 Sorabji, Philoponus and the Rejection of Aristotelian Science. 41
47 T.F. Torrance, Theological and Natural Science (Wipf & Stock Publishers,

effort to integrate reason and experience with one another in this world was of another class or kind utterly than had ever been fundamentally place upon by Aristotle and his followers. This is perhaps the most important reason why the great Alexandrian Scientist and Christian, John Philoponus, was so roundly condemned in his time and ultimately anathematized.

One must ask 'should Philoponus have been anathematised by the Church'? I think the problem in attempting to answer that question lies in the fact it was sensitive era, and going against the status quo was always going to ruffle some feathers. Yes, even if Philoponus may have held some alleged heretical views, I don't think it's too imperceptibly subtle to work out that other factors at involved – such as politics and authority were at play. It remains long established that anyone in a high position going against the norm will receive staunch criticism which may lead to higher end 'punishments', and perhaps this happened in the case of Philoponus. Regardless, I believe that one should not focus on his controversies and excommunication but rather his prevalent scientific and philosophical views that have influenced and impacted the whole world.

Although a controversial figure in his own time, Philoponus' independent philosophical ideas and Christian worldview permitted him to create a comprehensible system of thought that enabled argumentation and evidence to support his belief system, and be enriching to scientific discovery.[48] Philoponus made important intellectual contributions by criticising in detail the prevailing pagan view that the world must be eternal. He demonstrated flaws and opened the door for others to conceptualise other alternatives through his arguments. Had the pagan framework remained the only one available, it might have been impossible for western scientists to even conceive of

---

2005). https://books.google.com.au/books?id=PbJKAwAAQBAJ. 77
48 Ventureyra, Scott. "John Philoponus Contra Aristotle: The Emergence of Consciousness in Light of Contemporary Cosmology and Philosophy." Science Et Esprit , 2020. 153

Introduction

modern-day scientific theories, such as the belief that postulates the universe and time had a beginning.[49]

Philoponus' unrivalled analytical abilities, intellectual talent and his willingness to trust philosophical argument in doctrinal matters, made Philoponus shine out among his peers.[50] Philoponus was a good example demonstrating the nuance between philosophy and theology, giving rise to modern scientific theories. In this way, Philoponus exerted great influence both in his lifetime and beyond, though he was principally more successful as a philosopher and scientist than a theologian, while often being criticised for the latter. Philoponus should be given acclaim for being the first Christian theologian in the early church to take seriously the physics of the Cosmos in connection with the doctrines of the fathers, such as the doctrine of Athanasius, Cyril of Alexandria, and Severus of Antioch. Philoponus launched massive opposition to his Greek predecessor's views and appeal to authority, particularly Aristotle and Proclus, in order to elevate the status of Christianity as a standalone philosophical system. This is shown through looking at the entirety of his collected works. Philoponus believed that truth must not be judged by majority opinion or a number game. One of his most central contentions, deriving from his Orthodox Christian worldview, was that the matter of the universe had a beginning, and ultimately the Word of God become incarnate as a man among men in the Creation out of nothing in the beginning. No doubt the link between Philoponus' ideas and the scope of his innovation are remarkable, and this assessment remains largely uncontroversial and undisputed, however his

---

49 Couvalis, George. "John Philoponus: Closeted Christian or Radical Intellectual?" Modern Greek Studies Australia and New Zealand, 15: 207-219. A More Thorough Discussion of the Same Issues in French Is in Byzantinische Forschungen XXI 25-49, 2013., 2011. 217

50 Zachhuber, The Rise of Christian Theology and the End of Ancient Metaphysics: Patristic Philosophy from the Cappadocian Fathers to John of Damascus. 5

theological controversies and general disruptive force, has always seemed to surround him and haunted his ensuing influence.[51]

---

51 Sorabji, Philoponus and the Rejection of Aristotelian Science. 41

THE ARBITER
OR
THE WISE JUDGE

A PHILOSOPHICAL DEMONSTRATION
OF THE UNITY OF CHRIST

by: John Philoponus

Translated by Fr Robert Nixon, OSB

John Philoponus

Translator's Note

John Philoponus (c. 490–c. 570), also known as John the Grammarian and John of Alexandria, was one of the most distinguished scholars, philosophers and theologians of his times. His most widely circulated works have been his many commentaries on Aristotle, which were held in high esteem by thinkers as diverse as al-Ghazali, Avicenna, Averroes, Bonaventure, Pico della Mirandola, and Galileo.

His Christological writings are of particular interest and significance, and his masterpiece in this field is certainly his Arbiter (Διαιτητής), which is presented here in a new English translation. This wonderful treatise explores philosophically the implications of the union of Divinity and humanity in the Incarnate Christ. It is to be noted that the position which Philoponus articulates and defends is in perfect harmony with that of St. Cyril of Alexandria and the Council of Ephesus—namely that:

"The Word, in an unspeakable and inconceivable manner, united to Himself hypostatically a human body enlivened by a rational soul, and so became human and was called Son of Man. [...] Two different natures [thus] came together to form a unity, and from both arose one Christ, one Son. It was not as though the essence of the natures was destroyed by the union, but Divinity and humanity together made perfect for us one Lord and one Christ, together marvelously and mysteriously combining to form a unity."[52]

In the Arbiter, Philoponus, however, is not concerned with refuting the heresy of the Nestorians, who had already been

---

52 St. Cyril of Alexandria, Second Letter to Nestorius.

officially condemned about a century before he was writing. Rather, he aims at clarifying the theological language used to express the reality of the union of Divinity and humanity in Christ. In this endeavor, his skills as a philologist and philosopher shine through with radiant and illuminating clarity. He argues that what has been united is necessarily, and by definition, one. Christ is therefore one person, one hypostasis and one nature—but this one person, hypostasis and nature is both authentically Divine and authentically human.

It is interesting to note that the differences in terminology which are discussed in The Arbiter received much less attention in the Roman Catholic Church and in the Western Church in general, than in the Churches of the East. The reason for this is perhaps the fact that Nestorianism never had any significant impact in the West, and so the controversies which sprang up in the wake of its condemnation were likewise much less heated and topical. But there is nothing in the writings of Philoponus which is likely to raise any serious or substantial objections from most Roman Catholic theologians.

The text used in preparing the present translation is that contained in the volume Opuscula monophysitica Ioannis Philoponi, edited by Albert Sanda, and originally published in 1930. The English translation by Uwe Michael Lang offered in John Philoponus and the Controversies Over Chalcedon in the Sixth Century: A Study and Translation of the Arbiter has also been consulted. Apart from Lang's English translation, the text exists in Syriac and Latin versions (the original Greek version surviving only in isolated fragments). However, particular Greek philosophical terms are preserved in both the Syriac and the Latin versions.

In preparing this translation, every effort has been made to render the text accessible to the non-specialist (and in this respect, the result is quite different from Lang's highly literal version.) The long and complex sentence structures favored by Philoponus have often been broken up into several shorter and more comprehensible sentences. Technical philosophical expressions have been avoided as far as possible, and footnotes with definitions and explanations have been supplied whenever they seem helpful. The term "hypostasis" has been retained, but Philoponus himself explains the meaning and use of this word in detail during the course of his work. Texts contained in square brackets [.......] are editorial insertions, intended to complete or clarify the sense of the original.

It is the sincere hope of the translator that this work will both clarify the thought and assist the prayerful reflections of all who read it. I thank Fr. Anthony St. Shenouda for drawing my attention to the fascinating writings of John Philoponus, and Fr John St. Shenouda for his comprehensive and magisterial introduction. The Christological writings of Philoponus are deserving of renewed scholarly attention in our times, and this edition will certainly do much to make them accessible.

Translator's Note Bibliography

Lang, Uwe Michael. John Philoponus and the Controversies Over Chalcedon in the Sixth Century: A Study and Translation of the Arbiter. Spicilegium sacrum Lovaniense, Volume 47. Leuven: Peeters, 2001.

Sanda, Albert. Opuscula Monophystica Ioannis Philoponi. Beirut: Typographia Catholica PP. Soc. Jesu., 1930.

Prologue

For those who are able to see with clear eyes, the Truth itself always suffices as its own proof, and does not need else anyone to defend it. Yet there are, unfortunately, a great many things which darken people's vision of this Truth, and prevent them from coming to right judgment. For the uproar of personal conflict, greed, and ambition all make human beings biased in their judgment. In addition, people are often hesitant to change their opinions once they have formed them—so that they sometimes refuse to accept the clear truth, when it would entail them adopting a view which they have previously mocked or derided. In this way, the judgment of the human mind is readily made dull, sluggish, inflexible, and inert. Added to these factors is a lack of precision in the use of words and faulty logic, as well as mental laziness and stubbornness. All of these things are obstacles to people modifying their opinions, in response to sound arguments and demonstrations. Very often, they will prefer to stick firmly to their previous views, even when these clearly do not match with the truth.

We have encountered such vanity and folly in our human nature that it is enough to drive one to shed many tears! For if we are given a problem or question relating to some craft or field of science which we know nothing about, we are not ashamed to admit that we are ignorant of the answer. But in matters of theology, it is very much otherwise. Now, theology is surely the most difficult field of knowledge for any human being to master, and even consecrated priests are barely able to penetrate its subtle and arcane mysteries. Yet even people who have done no study in the field whatsoever, and who have (so to speak) barely dipped the tip of their finger into theology and Sacred Scripture, are embarrassed if they are not able to offer definite opinions (as if they were experts.) In doing this, they are acting as if they were the equals of those who have devoted their entire lives to such thing!

The only One who can purge our minds of this grave sickness is Christ, for He come to us in order to illuminate us with radiant light of Truth. Indeed, it is Christ alone, and no other, who has the power to do this.

Of those who engage in disputes today about the Incarnation of the Divine Word, most of them are really only arguing about the use of words, while the actual substance and content of their beliefs is virtually identical and indistinguishable. For all orthodox Christians believe in the union of the Divine Word with our human nature in the person of Christ. In truth, this great mystery surpasses what the human mind can understand; and yet it is essential and foundational to our faith, and is accepted without question by all Christians. There are some who say (quite rightly) that after this union, Christ had a single nature, which was both Divine and human. But there are others who insist that it is necessary to say that Christ had two natures after this union, rather than one.

Evidence that such differences arise more from the use of words than from the actual substance of faith is clear when one considers that such descriptions are normally used for the purpose of avoiding apparent paradoxes and logical inconsistencies. For those who insist on using the terminology of "two natures" are intent upon avoiding any suggestion of confusion of the Divinity and humanity, which were united in the person of Christ. Conversely, those who speak of "one nature" are seeking to avoid all traces of the Nestorian heresy.[53] This heresy denied the genuine union of

---

53 The Nestorian heresy originated from Nestorius (386-451), who denied the true union of Divinity and humanity in the person Christ. He argued that there was a kind of duality or division of nature in Jesus (sometimes characterized as the "two Sons" position), and expressed the view that Mary should not be called the "Mother of God" but only the "Mother of Christ." When Philoponus was writing, the views of Nestorius had already been officially condemned at the Council of Ephesus (431) about a century previously, and so were rejected by all orthodox Christians.

Divinity and humanity in the Incarnation of Christ, and reduced it to a mere "dwelling together" in the one body.

Those who use the terminology of 'two natures' from a supposed fear of confusion, say that they do not like to speak of 'one nature which is both Divine and human' for fear of negating the essential properties of either Divinity or humanity. Nevertheless, they accept the union of Divinity and humanity in the person of Jesus. Indeed, the very fear of absurdity which causes them to use such language is proof of their acceptance of the reality of this union of God and man in Christ.

Now this is exactly what you do not find in other heresies. For supporters of other heresies typically disparage the beliefs of those who hold the true faith. The treat the true Christians who disagree with them as wicked adversaries, and they do this merely for the sake of their own love of incessant arguing.

It seems to me that it is a sacred duty of a person who sincerely loves the truth of the faith to do whatever he can and to offer whatever arguments he may, so that dissentions and differences which pertain merely to words may be reconciled. For this reason, we have consented to the requests of those who have asked us to investigate this issue carefully, as far as our humble abilities permit. To do this, we shall adhere faithfully to the holy judgments of the tradition, and explain and defend these through sound arguments. In the end, supported by a fervent love of the truth, we hope to examine the statements advanced by our opponents [who insist upon the terminology of the 'two natures' of Christ], and to see honestly whether or not there is anything of right reason in them.

So that our proofs and argument may be more easily followed by those reading them, it is necessary firstly to lay down as a foundation two truths, which have been universally accepted by the common consent of all saints and holy authorities, and which, moreover, accord with Sacred Scripture. The first of these truths is that it was the eternal Son—the Only Begotten Word of the Father, true God from true God, and of one substance with His Father—who was made flesh through the holy Mother of God, the Virgin Mary, and thus became a genuine human being. The second truth is that there was no diminishment or mutation in His Divine nature in this Incarnation, but rather that He miraculously and perfectly united His unchanged Divinity with our human nature, including our physical body, rational mind, and intelligent soul.

And just as a human being is a union of a rational soul and a physical body, so the union of Divinity and humanity in Christ is integral and indissoluble. For the one Christ is the unique result of the union of the Divine Word and humanity. This is not a mere conjunction or agreement of two natures, as one might say [figuratively] that "a holy person has been united with God," or that "one person has been united to another person." Such expressions are normally used to describe a mere conjunction or agreement in purposes, and it is understood that the two natures remain separate and no single entity has emerged as a result conjunction—such as a new human person or living being. Rather, the union of Divinity and humanity in Christ is comparable to the union of the body and rational soul, which constitutes a single, complete human being. In Christ, the Divine Word, having been perfectly united to humanity nature, comes to direct it, in the same way in which the rational soul of a human being directs the body of the same human being. But, just as in a human person, the result of the union of body and rational soul is a single, integral being; so, through the Incarnation, a single, integral Christ is the result of the perfect union of the Divine Word and humanity. In Christ, the Divinity is the moving principle. This Divinity works through His rational soul, and is then brought to fulfilment in His physical body.

Thus, the union of natures which took place in Christ was much more profound and complete than the union of elements (i.e., rational soul and physical body) which takes place in every human being. For in human beings, there are certain movement and impulses which take their origin from our physical body only, rather than our rational soul. And our rational soul moves the body only in the range of movements which are described as "voluntary." For the rational soul of a human being is not able to direct each and every movement of the body. For example, if our body should happen to fall from a great height and plummet to the ground, the rational soul is not able to stop its movement downwards. Or if the body is afflicted by a fever, the rational soul is not able to direct the body to become cool again. For our rational soul have no control over those actions which pertain only to our body as a physical object. Therefore, the union of the rational soul with the body in a human being is imperfect, since there are numerous matters in which the rational human soul has no say at all [such as feelings of pain, hunger, fatigue, etc.] It is therefore true to say that certain actions and events pertain to the physical body alone.

But in the case of Our Lord Jesus Christ, since Divinity is (by its very nature) omnipotent and all-encompassing, all that pertained to the person of Christ was directed by His Divinity. Everything which He did, and everything which happened to Him, happened in accordance with the omnipotent will of His Divinity. Therefore, the Divine will, which was communicated by means of His rational soul, was carried out perfectly and completely in His physical body.

In an ordinary human being, it is not possible to divide certain of our actions (such as speaking, smelling, seeing and hearing) between the body and soul, for they pertain to the whole human being. In an analogous but broader manner, it is not possible to divide any of the actions or experiences of Christ between His Divinity and his humanity. For, as has been shown, all of His actions and experiences—physical, mental and emotional—were necessarily subject to His Divinity. Thus, when we consider Christ, we cannot say that His action in something like walking pertained only to His physical body, or that His fulfilment of the requirements of justice related only to His rational soul or human nature. Rather, all of the actions and experiences of Christ belong to His single nature. This single nature was directed by His Divinity, and mediated by His rational soul, and carried out by His physical body.

The sufferings which Christ experienced, as a result of the fragility of His mortal body, were a sign of and witness to the reality of His Incarnation. Again, these sufferings are rightly attributed to His whole person, for they did not occur except by the consent of the Divine Word. When we speak of human beings, we may say, "Peter or Paul is sick or injured. It is his body which suffers!" And there are other passions or disturbances which draw their origin from the rational soul, such as the experience of uncertainty, or weariness, or anxiety, of love, or hate. For all of these feelings seem to relate to the rational soul, more than the physical body. Nonetheless, it is correct to say that all human feelings (whether drawing their origin from the physical body or from the rational soul) are experienced by the "whole person," since a whole person is essentially a union of the rational soul and the physical body.

Furthermore, what makes us human beings is the fact that we possess a rational soul. As for the physical body, other forms of animal life also possess physical bodies, with similar physical senses, limbs, and organs. So we are called "human beings" because of the rational soul which we possess, for the possession of a rational soul is what distinguishes human beings from other animals. It is the same with Christ; for it is the unique element in the union (namely, His Divinity) which makes Him to be Christ, rather than just an ordinary human being. Hence Christ is correctly called "God," on account of His perfect and unique Divinity.

Now, returning to the case of ordinary human beings, they are sometime referred to on the basis of the lower element in the union which forms them. Sometimes we may refer to human beings as "flesh" [such as in the expression "the way of all flesh..."] In a similar way, Christ is often referred to as "man" or "the Son of Man." But this is always to be understood as referring to the entire Christ, who is both Divine and human. For just as Scripture often calls human beings "flesh," so it should not surprise us if its sometimes refers to Christ as "man."

Therefore no one should be offended to find Our Lord sometimes referred to as "a man", rather than "God" or "Great God" or "God over all" or "the God of the ages" or "the Creator of things visible and invisible" or "He from Whom all things draw existence." And whenever we read Scriptures referring to Christ as "God", we should understand this to include His humanity as well. Likewise, whenever we read the Scriptures referring to Him as "a man," we should understand that also to encompass His Divinity.

Now that we have professed accurately what is commonly believed about Christ by all people who sense things in a religious and orthodox manner, we will next investigate each of these points in more detail. [For example,] is it correct to say that there is one single, composite nature in Christ after the union of Divinity and humanity in His person; or should we say instead that there are two natures, or that He was "manifested in two natures"?

When we speak of the union of Divine Word with the flesh in Christ, we are not speaking of it as if it was something eternally existing. Rather, this union was something which took place at a particular point in time, in the mystery of the Incarnation. In the same way, when we speak of a garment being whitened, or brass being made by mixing metals together, the union takes place at a definite point in time, although the elements may have existed beforehand. Now, with Christ, the Divine Word existed long before its union with humanity, and, in fact, existed eternally. This is in accordance with the practice of Christians to refer to "the one nature of Christ, after the union of Divinity and humanity." And it is understood that this one nature is composite, i.e., both Divine and human.

Chapter I

If we believe in the union of the Divinity and humanity of Christ, and that this union is not confined only to particular properties (such as honor, or power, or works, etc.) but rather pertains to their very essence (for such indeed is implied in a genuine union), we may then ask ourselves, "Does this mean there is a single nature which results from this? Yes, or no?"

If we do not say that one nature resulted, how can we then claim that the union was genuine? For the very meaning of the word "union" is for things to be made one. In the case of the prophets, though they were inspired by God, we do not speak of any actual "union" of them with God. [Thus the case of the union of God and humanity in Christ is utterly unique. For in Him alone did such a union occur.]

[But does this union, upon which all orthodox Christians agree, necessarily mean that Divinity and humanity became truly one in Christ? Let us examine the question logically.] When we speaking of something as being "whitened," we mean that it attains whiteness and the condition of being white. And when we speak of something as being "heated", we mean that it attains heat and the condition of being hot. In a similar way, when we speak of a "union", we mean that what participates in the union attains unity and the condition of being one.

The Divine Scriptures do not cease to proclaim that "the Word became flesh,"[54] and therefore has been made Incarnate. But, out of respect for piety in these holy mysteries, it is judicious to note that the statement "the Word became flesh" is not precisely like saying "this object was made white," or "that object was heated up." For in those cases, it is an external force which imbues some property to the object acted upon. In contrast, the

---

54 John 1:14

Incarnation of the Divine Word means that this Divine Word itself was united to flesh, such that a single, living Christ was the result. The Divine Essence was not in itself changed through this Incarnation or acted upon by an external agent, as if God was being enclosed within a body, or being transformed into a body.

It is appropriate that Scripture uses the expression "becoming flesh", rather than simply "becoming one with humanity." For "becoming one" is often used metaphorically to indicate simply an agreement and concord of feelings and affections. We even find this sense to be used in Scripture, such as when Christ prays to the Father, "I pray that they may all be one in us."[55] So, the use of the expression "made flesh" guards against any misinterpretation of the union of Divinity and humanity, as if it meant merely an agreement of feelings and affections, while the two natures remained separate. For how can there be any ambiguity about the true and genuine nature of the union which is expressed in the declaration that "the Word became flesh"? How could our minds imagine that there remains any essential division that which has been so truly united?

If therefore (as I have said) the effect of a true union of natures is to produce a single One, what, then, is this One? Is it a mere name, or is it a reality? If it is a mere name and not a reality, then there was no genuine union at all [but merely a nominal or conceptual one.]. Thus it is that we call a constellation of stars "the Dog" (also known as "Orion"), and we also call a regular, earthly dog by the same name. But this unity or likeness between the constellation and an ordinary canine is merely nominal. For in essence they are not united at all. And similarly, we may have a painted picture of a human being [of which we may say: "That is a human being", but really meaning "that is a picture of a human being,"] and also an actual human being. But though we may call them both by the same name, they are not of the same essence.

---

55 John 7:21.

Chapter I

But if two natures are really united in such a way that they are made one in being, then the union is one of reality, and not merely a union of name. And if it is a real "union" then, by definition, the outcome is necessarily "one."

Now, there is a unity of nature or essence, and there is also a unity of the appearances or properties which pertain to the respective nature or essence. But if it is a unity which pertains only too appearances, while the essences or natures remains separate, it is not really a union, but rather a kind of conjunction. And this is what the Nestorians believe. For the say, "In as much as the human being who was born of Mary has shared the honor, work and power of the Divine Word, one single name may be given [to both this human being and to the Divine Word which worked through him.]"

But our present work is not directed at corrected the patently absurd heresy of the Nestorians. Rather, we simply demonstrate that the union of Divine and human nature in Christ was not a question of appearances (and therefore nominal), as the Nestorians say. Rather, it is a true union, which pertains to essence or nature.

We should point out that these two terms, "essence" and "nature," refer [in practice] to the same thing. And it is a union (or "making one") of essence or nature which took place in Christ. Thus it is correct to say that, as a consequence of the Incarnation, Our Lord Jesus Christ was of one nature—a nature which was both human and Divine.

There are those who assert that we should not say "one nature," but "one Christ who is the result of the union of two natures." I would say to such people, "Tell me, does the word "Christ" (which is given to the Incarnate Word of God) signify an essence or nature, or merely an appearance or set of actions?" Now, if the answer is the latter (i.e., only an appearance or set of actions) then, as has been shown above, no union of natures has taken place all, but only a kind of conjunction or co-operation. But it is agreed among all orthodox Christians that the Incarnation was a genuine union of Divinity and humanity—that is to say, of Divine nature (or essence) and of human nature (or essence).

Therefore, the term "Christ" must pertain to essence or nature (i.e., that which is constitutive of the identity of an entity), rather than merely an appearance or set of actions. And if the name "Christ" refers to essence or nature, there are two possibilities which can be raised. Does it speak of one essence or nature, or two? If it speaks of one nature, this nature (as I have demonstrated) is both Divine and human. But if it speaks of two natures, it either speaks of each one individually, or of both natures collectively. Now, if it speaks of two natures separately, one would be bound to say that there are two Christs! But even if it speaks of both collectively (in the same way that we may say that both Peter and Paul together are "a pair of men"), we would still fall into the absurdity of saying that there are two Christs.

But we know that there are not two Christs, but only One, both in name and in substance! Now, if (as has been shown) the name "Christ" must pertain to a nature or essence, it follows that this unique Christ is of one, unique nature [which is both Divine and human.] To maintain that the name "Christ" signifies two natures (which may each be considered separately) is to fall into an error which would please Nestorius!

To speculate that the name of "Christ" may refer to two natures collectively is also a manifest error. For it refers to the product of the union of these two natures, not the two natures collectively. In a similar way, when we speak of a "human being," we are not referring to the rational soul and physical body as a kind of set of two things, but rather we are speaking of the union of the two, which is what a human being is. Or when we speak of a "house," we are not speaking of the stones and wood which went into making the house as a kind of collection of objects in the same location, but rather of the single entity [the house] which is the result of their union. The term "choir" also is not a collective noun, encompassing many individual singers who happen to be randomly gathered together, but rather it describes a single, organized ensemble, formed from these many singers. These examples of singular names only make sense when a single entity is being spoken of, even if that entity if formed from numerous elements.

But there are those who say that the single name "Christ" speaks of the "end-product" of two natures (Divine and human) being united. But then, one may well ask what precisely this "end-product" is? Is it a mere name, or is it a reality? And if it is a reality, it is either an essence or nature, or an appearance or action pertaining to an essence or nature. But the absurdity in imaging that it is a mere appearance or action, rather than an actual nature or essence, has already been demonstrated. And because it must be a single essence or nature which is designated by the singular name of "Christ," it follows that Christ is a single nature! And so Christ, who is unique and One, is of only one nature.

But it is equally evident that this nature is composite [being simultaneously both Divine and human], in the same way that a human being, though truly having one nature, is a composite of a rational soul and physical body.

There are those who assert that it is right to describe Christ as being one "hypostasis," but maintain that it does not follow that He has only one nature. [Later in this work] we shall consider this proposition, and demonstrate that it is self-contradictory, and saying something which is simply not possible.

I am also not unaware that some learned people have pointed out that the term "Christ" (Christos) does not refer to an essence or nature at all, but of an action performed upon an essence or nature. For the original meaning of Christos was "one who is anointed," or "having been anointed." Technically, this is true. And the same may be said of other designations, which do not in themselves describe a person, but rather they describe some action which the person performs, such as "king," "grammarian," "philosopher," "master", or "servant." Nevertheless, we do regularly and customarily use such designations to refer to the person themselves—speaking of their essence and nature, and not just the role indicated by their title. For when we say, "The King has arrived," we are speaking of a particular person of a certain nature, not a royal rank in an abstract or generic sense. In the same way, if we say: "The grammarian walks (or sleeps, or is sick)," we mean that an actual person does this, not that the field of knowledge relating to grammar performs this activity (which would be absurd!) Instead, the person is designated by the profession or role they happen to undertake.

[It is the same in the case of Christ.] Thus it was when Peter declared to Jesus: "You are the Christ, the Son of the living God!"[56] What else did he means here by the expression "Christ" than "the One who is by nature the Son of the living God"? Therefore, although the word "Christ" ("christos") originally referred to an action (of having been anointed) it came to refer to a single definite person and a single definite nature. For it is ridiculous to think that the union of Divine and human nature should result in an action rather than an entity, i.e., something which pertains to a nature rather than a nature itself!

Rather, in believing that the name "Christ" signifies a single nature (which is a composite of Divinity and humanity), we are speaking according to the truth of our faith, and neither do we stray from what is strictly logical.

---

56 Matthew 16:6

Chapter II

There are two natures which are united in Christ (and these two natures are the same as "essences"); one of these is Divine and the other is human. From this, two possibilities then follow: either Christ is the same as the natures which are brought into union in Him, or He is different from them. If Christ is different from these Divine and human natures which are united in Him, the question is then arises: what is He, since He is held to be different from the Divinity and humanity which are in union in Him?

But this is entirely impossible! For nothing that exists is different from its own constitutive nature or essence. As an example, the nature of a human being is a "rational, mortal animal." For this is the universally accepted definition of a human being, and definitions of things do nothing but identify or signify their essence or natures. So if a human being was different from this human nature, it would mean that he would not be a "rational, mortal animal." But a human being is, by definition, a rational, mortal animal. How then could a human being be other than a rational, mortal animal? [This would mean that a human being was not a human being, which is plainly absurd.]

Similarly, if Christ were something different from His nature (that is, both Divine and human), Christ would be something different from Christ—which is likewise absurd and ridiculous! Thus clearly Christ is not other than His nature or essence.

This also proves that the nature of Christ is truly one. For if we hypothesize that He had two natures, and that He was the same as each of these two natures (which is necessarily the case, since we have demonstrated that nothing can be other than its nature), then there must be two Christs (as Nestorius asserts), and not one Christ (as Sacred Scripture clearly shows). But since there is one Christ only, both in name and in reality, then there is only one nature in Christ.

Similarly, since there is only one sun, there must be only one "nature of the sun." For even if diverse properties may be observed in the sun (such as brightness or heat, a spherical shape, circular motion, and so forth) there is no need to say that the sun has more than one nature. For no single particular characteristic or property is, in itself, the nature of the sun. For example, brightness is a property of the sun, but it is not its nature—for fire also exhibits brightness. And a spherical shape is a property of the sun, but is not its nature—for many other objects also possess a spherical shape. The same applies with circular motion, and any other property one may perceive in the sun. But the unique combination of all these properties (brightness, heat, spherical shape, circular motion, and many others) together form the particular nature of the sun. And since the sun is unique, its nature is also unique.

It is the same in the case of Christ, the God-man. Though He exhibits properties which are both Divine and human, those who judge rightly will not assert from this that He has two natures. For the nature of Christ is not either of these on its own and in isolation; it is neither His Divinity without His humanity, nor His humanity without His Divinity. Rather, His unique nature is the outcome of the union of both. He is one being and not two, and therefore we profess one Christ, who has one nature. But this nature, as we have often noted before, is a union of Divinity and humanity.

Chapter III

The name of "Christ", which we use to speak of Our Savior, does not signify only His Divinity or only His humanity, but both together. We may then ask if this name, "Christ," signifies an essence or nature, or merely features and properties which belong to an essence or nature. If it signifies the latter only (features or properties, but not a single nature) than these must be the incidental result of the conjunction of cohesion of two natures [the Divine and the human,] and not a union. For if both the Divinity and humanity of Christ remain as two separate [albeit co-operating] natures after the Incarnation, then there was merely a conjunction or cohesion of the two, rather than a true union.

Such a conjunction of cohesion (if we imagine it to be the case) would be comparable to that which can be observed in a choir, or house, or city, or such things. The various elements of these examples are said to be united. But such a so-called union is really a cohesion or conjunction, for the nature of the individual members remains separate, when they are considered in themselves. A choir is a good example, for the term signifies a single phenomenon or activity, resulting from the conjunction of a multiplicity of singers. However, this conjunction does not prevent the individual singers from continuing to have their own separate essences and natures. The same may be said of a house. For the building which we call a "house" is a construction or conjunction of wood and stone and other substances. But the wood and stone and all the other materials involved retain their own individual essences, and continue to have separate natures. Thus terms like "chorus" and "house," though technically not collective nouns, refer to a conjunction or set of relationships, rather than a substance or entity in itself. For the separate natures of the constituent elements of these continue in their multiplicity of natures.

[But since the name of "Christ" refers to a genuine person, not merely a juxtaposition of conjunction of elements,] it is clear that it does not designate merely properties, features, or activities pertaining to a nature (or a relationship between natures), but a nature itself.

It is well known that nouns (or "naming words") may function in different ways. For example, they can be used univocally. This means that they identify one nature or essence in an unambiguous way, but are applicable to all particular entities or examples of that nature or essence. An example of this is the normal usage of the word "horse," meaning a terrestrial quadruped of the equine genus. Any creature which has this nature or essence is called a horse, such as (for example) a horse owned by Xanthos, or a horse owned by Balios, etc. In this sense, the word "horse" identifies one essential nature, although it may be applied to a great many individual entities which have this nature.

A noun may also sometimes by used as a homonymously. [6] This means that the one and the same word is applied to more than one nature or essence. Again, the word "horse" can be used to illustrate this. For we may speak of a "sea horse," as well as land horse. Of course, when we call an entity a "sea horse" we are not speaking of the same essential nature as that of a land horse. Though the same name is used, the same essential nature is not being designated. The meaning is, however, generally clear from the context of usage. In any given context, a noun (even if it is a

---

6 A homonym is a word which has more than one meaning, without changing its sound or spelling. An example of this would be the word "glasses," which could mean either a pair of spectacles to assist vision, or receptacles used to contain beverages. But, according to Philoponus, when the word is used in any given context, it carries only one of these two possible meanings. Thus if a person says, "I need glasses to read," he is speaking of a pair of spectacles. On the other hand, if a person says, "I will pour your drinks into glasses," he is clearly meaning receptacles for beverages. In both cases, the word signifies only one nature, and does not include the alternative, homonymous meaning.

homonym) properly designates only one single nature or essence. Thus, if person speaks of himself as "having ridden a horse," it is evident that he is using the word to designate an entity with the nature and essence of a land horse, [and not a sea horse!]

Now, in the case of nouns, even those which refer to a class of entities with the same nature or essence, it is evident that they are often used to speak of particular, individual beings. For example, if I am speaking of a certain individual (say Peter or Paul) and refer to him as "the man", I mean only one definite person. And if I am speaking of a particular horse or ox, when I use the word "the horse" or "the ox" it is understood to be speaking of this individual entity, not of the class of animals of that species in general. Hence when we say that there are many (or few) men in a city, we are speaking of the individual entities belonging to this class. We are not speaking in general of the class of entities who exhibit a particular nature or essence [as is done in a statement like, "Man is rational animal,"] but of individual, singular persons. Otherwise, how could we say that there are many or few?

[Similarly, when the term "man" is used to refer to the entire class of beings, it still refers to one nature only, although this nature is common to many. In either case, the single noun designates a single nature, whether it is individual or collective.]

Our discussion has thus proved that any noun or name signifies one nature only, if it is properly understood in its particular context. So it is with the name of "Christ." For this word, Christos ("anointed"), is sometimes used homonymously; that is, it is occasionally used to describe a prophet or a king in the Old Testament, and at other times—indeed, in the vast majority of cases—it is used to indicate the person of Jesus Christ) But when we use this title to speak of Our Savior, clearly only one single individual is actually meant—that is, He in whom Divinity and humanity were perfectly united, and who is Son both of God and Mary. And, as has been shown, this term applies not to just to the properties and attributes pertaining to this Savior, but to the person of the Savior Himself, in His very nature and essence.

Thus, the single term "Christ," when used as a title for the unique Son of God, necessarily designates only a single nature (as is the case of every noun, when it is properly understood in its context). And since it refers to He in whom Divinity and humanity were perfectly united, it follows that Christ, the God-man, has a single nature [which is, as has been frequently noted, simultaneously both human and Divine.]

Chapter IV

If duality (that is, the condition of being two) indicates and originates from a division of a unity, then, for things to be "two" means that they exist in a state of separation from unity, and that there is a division between the things which are enumerated as being two. But such a division is in essential opposition to unity. Hence it is obvious than nothing can be simultaneously "two" and "one." Insofar as things are two, they cannot also be one; or at least, not in the same respect that they are being counted as two.

I have said "insofar as things are two" intentionally. To give an example, two people—say, Peter and Paul—are two, insofar as they are the separate persons of Peter and Paul. But they may be regarded as united (or "one") in some other respect. For instance, they are both rational, mortal beings, as so are both members of the human race. In this regarded, they may be said to be united, and are "one" in respect to their species. But insofar as one is Peter and the other is Paul, they are clearly two, for indeed these are individual names or "proper nouns," pertaining to separate natures. They may be united in the sense that they both belong to the same species, i.e., they are both human beings. But they are not united in the sense that one is the individual person, Peter, and the other is the individual person, Paul.

For human nature (in an abstract sense) may be said to be one. But this nature is shared by many individuals, who partake of this nature. The same may be said of a ship, which is one in the sense that it is a single ship. And the many components and parts of this ship are united, in the sense that they are all parts of this ship. But they are many, insofar as they retain their own individual natures (whether as wood, or nails, or ropes.)

Similarly for a teacher, delivering a lesson. He may teach a single lesson, but this lesson is received by many individual students. So he has taught one single lesson in a certain sense, but in another sense has taught as many lessons as he has students. And the same may be said of a sigil ring. The ring contains only one seal, but this seal may be stamped upon many documents. Again, in a sense the seal is only one, but in another sense it is many (insofar as it has been stamped onto many documents).

And there is yet another case which should be noted. A plank of wood may be said to be two cubits in length. Now, although it is said to be "two cubits", it is only one, single object. In describing the piece of wood as being "two cubits," what is really being said is that it has the potential to be divided into two pieces, each of one cubit's length. [Thus once again, the duality, or notion of "twoness," implies a division or potential division.]

If all of this is true, and if there are really two natures in Christ (as some claim), then it is obvious that these two are not a unity. If there were two natures in Christ, these two natures are [by definition] not also one—that is to say, they are not united. In whatever respect they are considered two (or divided), they cannot also be considered one (or united.) But if there really were two natures in Christ (that is, one Divine and one human), they would be even more divided than the aforementioned example of the two men, Peter and Paul. For these two hypothetical men are at least of the same species. They are one and united, at least insofar as their unity of species is considered. But Divinity and humanity are not of the same species or genre. Rather, they are are fundamentally and incommensurably different. So Divinity and humanity cannot be considered "one," except by virtue of a supernatural or miraculous union.

Indeed, the Divine nature utterly transcends all that has been brought into existence through its omnipotence! Although we sometimes apply words to God, and talk about His "existence" or "essence," His reality far surpasses all the concepts designated by such words. Thus God cannot be said to be "united" to humanity in respect of being of the same species, of genus, or sharing any property or attribute in common at all. God, who is utterly transcendent, is united to humanity only by the miraculous, ineffable and indivisible union in the Incarnation of Christ. This union is not a mere commonality of attributes, but a union of nature, substance and being, in the sacred person of Christ. And if these natures (Divinity and humanity) are so wondrously united in Christ, it is absurd to maintain that these natures were still divided in Him.

Now, if there is no division in the nature of Christ (since a division is evidently contradictory to a union of natures, which is fundamental to our faith), then there cannot be duality (or twoness) cannot either. For if something does not have color, evidently it does not whiteness. If something is not a living being, evidently it cannot be a human being. And if something does not have division, evidently it cannot be two (or any other number, apart from one.) If there is no division in the nature of Christ [which would be contradictory to the union of Divinity and humanity in Him, which our faith universally affirms], then there cannot be twoness, or multiplicity, or anything other than unity. Hence it is only right that we profess Christ to have one nature, which is both Divine and human.

This one nature of Christ may encompass many particular powers and properties; just as a fire, though of one nature, exhibits heat and brightness and redness and lightness. It is certainly no wondrous or strange thing if one nature and one entity exhibits a multitude of different attributes and properties. For indeed, the human body, though one, has a range of different features and powers in its various components.

Why, then, should anyone consider it impossible for the varied features and powers of Christ to pertain to His one nature? Are His various aspects or properties [such as His Divinity and humanity] still divided? But all those who profess that there is one Christ must also necessarily accept a union, [which precludes division.].

Indeed, those who profess an undivided union of natures in Christ [which is to say, all orthodox Christians] must, as a logical consequence, profess that He has one nature. For the individual in whom these natures are united, and who is the result of this wonderful union of God and man, is one, the Holy One who is called "Christ."

Chapter V

If it is recognized that the Incarnate Christ is a single nature, formed from the union of Divinity and humanity, then His nature is composite—that is, it is composed from, and includes, both Divinity and humanity. This is analogous to the case of a human being, who is a composite nature comprising both physical body and rational soul.

But if it is insisted upon that He has two natures, then the question arises, "Are these two natures simple, or are they composite?" [And the attempt to answer this question gives rise to many logical absurdities.] For if one says that Christ has two simple natures, a problem at once emerges. For the Divinity and humanity of which He is composed are both simple natures. To say that two simple natures are the result of the union of two simple natures is clearly absurd. For if that were the case, the union has had no effect whatsoever and is of no significance. And any nature which is the result of the union of two simple natures is (by definition) composite, and not simple. This is the very meaning of the term "composite."

On the other hand, it is equally absurd to say that two composite natures are the result of the union of two simple natures. For any composite nature, by definition, includes more than one simple nature—that is to say, it requires at least two. How, then, could the union of two simple natures give rise to two composite natures? Since each composite nature requires the participation of at least two simple natures, to form two composite natures from two simple natures is simply not possible.

Thus, if any cares to argue that Christ has two natures, let him specify whether he means two simple natures or two composite natures. But each of these possibilities has been shown to be impossible and absurd. For the only logical outcome of the union of two simple natures [that is, Divinity and humanity] is one, composite nature.

Chapter VI

Christ is indeed one, both in name and in reality, for there are not two Christs. A person could then consider what is the best answer to give for someone wishes to define Him, or how to give a simple response to the question: "Who is Christ?" [Although such a definition would be difficult, in principle it should be possible to answer such a question in a meaningful and satisfactory way, or at least to form a mental concept of what is meant be the term "Christ," when used as a designation for Our Savior. A possible definition might be: "Jesus, who is the unique Only Begotten Son of God, in whom Divinity and humanity are perfectly united."]

Now, any definition of a person or thing signifies their nature. And the same applies to Christ. Although a definition may include several elements [such as that proposed above], it nevertheless signifies one nature only.

Now, if Christ had two natures, it would be necessary to supply two definitions. And each of these two definitions would describe a different subject or entity—that is, one or the other of these two natures. But this is absurd, because every entity has only a single correct definition, and the one Christ (likewise) cannot correctly have two separate and distinct definitions—that is to say, two definitions which are different or mutually incompatible, insofar as they refer to different entities. [A multitude of different attributes or titles may indeed be given to Christ, but they all refer to the one subject—that is, Christ Himself—and therefore they are really elements, or possible elements, of one definition.]

And, since Christ (being a single entity) cannot have two separate definitions, He cannot have two natures either! For every definition describes a single nature only, whether this nature is simple or composite.[7]

---

[7] The argument advanced in this very short chapter is admittedly a little difficult to follow for contemporary readers. It may be summarized as follows: since Christ is a definite and specific person, it must be possible to identify Him by means of a description of His essential nature (or to "define" or identify who Christ is.) Since such a definition would serve to identify or describe His nature, it follows that He (as a single, identifiable entity) must also have a single, definite nature. If this were not the case, it would be impossible to answer the question, "Who is Christ?", in any meaningful or comprehensible way.

Chapter VII

Our seventh chapter will consider a position adopted by many of those who assert that Christ does not have one nature. They claim that, though there is only one hypostasis[8] in Christ, there are still two natures. In asserting this position, they repudiate those who hold that He has one nature, and also repudiate those who assert that He has two hypostases.

But before we undertake to disprove this view, it is necessary to consider exactly what the Church means by the terms "nature" and "hypostasis," as well as the related expression "person." A "nature" is understood to be the essence of a thing or class of things, [which corresponds with its definition.] An example might be to say that the nature of a human being is a mortal, rational, living creature, capable of reason and understanding. For these properties are common to all human beings, and what distinguish human beings from other living entities. It is to be noted that "substance," "essence," and "nature" are effectively identical and interchangeable.

The term "hypostasis" means a particular, concrete example of any given nature. Now, particular examples of any nature may vary from each other, in respect to certain individual properties or characteristics. In the practice of the Church, these individual realizations of a nature are known as hypostases, and also [for human beings, and in some other cases] as persons. The philosophers of the school of Aristotle also call them "individuals."

Considering how natures and individuals are classified, living things can be divided into the categories of rational and irrational living creatures. Now, the category of rational creatures can be divided up further, into the classes of humans, angels and

---

8 Philoponus will speak of the meaning of this philosophical term in the following paragraphs.

demons. The Aristotelian philosophers call particular cases of these categories or classes "individuals"—so that Peter and Paul (for example) are individual human beings, and St. Michael and St. Gabriel are individual angels. This term "individual" literally means an entity which cannot be divided further, that is "indivisible." To take the case of a human individual, if he or she were to be divided up (say, the body and the soul separated from each other) they would cease to be a human being!

The Church applies this philosophical terminology to theological matters. For example, the Father, the Son, and the Holy Spirit are each of the same nature (that is, they are each Divine.) Yet they are three separate hypostases, or individual "persons." For the Father, Son, and Holy Spirit are each distinguished from each other by particular properties, yet all are, both in common and individually, Divine (or God).

The implication of this is that the Divine nature is what is common to each of these hypostases, rather than what distinguishes the various members or persons of the Trinity from each other. Yet, in speaking of a "nature," this term is also sometimes used to designate one particular individual [as we have demonstrated in Chapter III.] For we might say "the man," when speaking, not of human beings in general, but about a particular hypostasis or person, such as Peter or Paul. Similarly, when we speak of the union of the Divine and human natures in the Incarnation, we are not speaking of the Divine persons (i.e., the members of the Holy Trinity) in a general sense. For it was only the particular hypostasis of the Word (that is, the Son) who was made flesh and thereby united to humanity. And similarly, when we say that God the Son was "united to humanity," we do not mean He was united only in a general or collective sense to human nature, but rather was united in the individual person of Christ.

Thus it is that when we speak of the "union of Divine nature and human nature" in Christ, the union pertains to a particular person or hypostasis. Thus "nature" and "hypostasis" in this particular context signify the exactly same reality, for the nature referred to is a particular nature, i.e., the nature of a single hypostasis. Hence it is that many people speak of the "union of Divine nature and human nature" in Christ as a "hypostatic union," treating the terms nature and hypostasis as effectively interchangeable. [And, in this context, they indeed are.]

It should be further noted that the term "person" is often used interchangeably with "hypostasis." For example, we may speak of the "three persons" of the Holy Trinity, or the "three hypostases," meaning exactly the same thing.

Proof that the terms "nature" and "hypostasis" are used to designate exactly the same things when speaking of the union of God and man in Christ can be found by considering the terms which the Nestorians use. For they assert that Christ had two natures and also two hypostases, [evidently understanding nature and hypostasis to mean the same thing in this context]. However, they say that Christ was "one person." It is their belief that the Son born of Mary was a mere human being, who received a Divine illumination. His illumination (they say) was complete, and it is in this respect that He was different from the various prophets, who each received only a partial illumination. They say that the name "Christ" actually designates the unique relationship (not union) of Divine and human natures (or hypostases) which took place in the human Son, born of Mary. It is, they say, this relationship which is one—although the participants in this relationship (the Divine Word and the man Jesus) are not one, but two.

But for those who do not subscribe to the wicked heresy of Nestorius, the expressions of the "one hypostasis" and the "one person" of Christ indicates the same thing, and such terms may be used indifferently and interchangeably, since they convey the same meaning.

It is to be noted that there was not a single instant when Jesus, the human being, existed without being in union with the Divine

Word, and therefore the humanity of Christ never existed apart from His Divinity. The Divine nature (in the hypostasis of the Word) and human nature (in the hypostasis of Jesus) were thus united concurrently, at the moment of the conception of Jesus. [And from this union, the one person, nature, and hypostasis of the Incarnate Christ, entered this world.]

Now, for those who claim that Christ had two natures but one hypostasis, a problem immediately arises. For (as I have shown) the union of Divinity and humanity in Christ necessarily pertained to nature and hypostasis, equally and inseparably. To those who say that Christ had one hypostasis but two natures, I ask them this: Are they saying that the hypostases of the Divine Word and the human being Jesus were more united, but that somehow the Divine and human natures were less united? Such a proposition is untenable, because union and unity does not admit of such varying degree. The Divine and human hypostases and natures were either united in Christ, or they were not. There is no "more" or "less" in a union, more so than two plus three can produce any other result than five!

"But", some may argue, "things can be more or less united. If two things of the same species—such as two drops of water or two pieces of wood—are united, they are more united, than if two things which differ in species of genus—such as the soul and the body—are united." But this objection does not serve to clarify why the Divine and human hypostases should be more completely united than the Divine and human natures. After all, it is evident that the same degree of the possibility of union [or "unitability"] exists between hypostasis and hypostasis, and nature and nature.

But there are those who wish to defend their position by saying that they wish to use the language of "one hypostasis and two natures" to preserve the idea of union (in the expression "one hypostasis"), but also to guard against the possibility of any intermixture. And they guard against the possibility of implying any intermixture by using—so they say—the expression "two natures."

But it is absurd to profess a union, and at the same time to wish to assert an absence of "intermixture." And this fear of suggesting any intermixture is misguided and unfounded. For an intermixture does not necessarily imply any loss of particular properties. The Divine nature, though "intermixed" with human nature, does not cease to be Divine; nor does the human nature cease in any way to be human.

Furthermore, it is inconsistent to accept a union (and therefore an intermixture) of the hypostases of the Divine Word and the person of Jesus; but to reject an intermixture of their natures. If the hypostases become one, surely it is absurd to object to the natures becoming one. But if it is acceptable to declare that the union of Divinity and humanity produced one hypostasis in Christ, surely it is equally acceptable to declare that they produced one nature (that is both Divine and human.)

The expression "one hypostasis but two natures" has led more people astray than any other [in discussions of this question.] Indeed, it is an expression that is in part true (in professing "one hypostasis.") But it is inconsistent and self-contradictory.

Moreover, it should be noted that, while it is possible for hypostases to exceed natures in number, it is not possible for natures to exceed hypostases. For any one nature can be manifested in a number of hypostases. An example of this is the Holy Trinity itself, where this is one Divine nature, but three Divine hypostasis. Another example is human beings. For there is one human nature, but many individual hypostases of this nature, in the multitude of individual persons who exist. And any number of similar examples could be provided. [Thus it is that natures, being the broader category, cannot be greater in number than hypostases, which are the individual instances of these natures.]

It therefore cannot be the case that two natures should together from one hypostasis. This is readily shown by considering any number other example: such as, how could the two natures of stone and wood be present in a single substance, or how could the nature of an ox and a horse be present in the same individual animal, or (for that matter) how could the two distinct natures of God and man be present in the same person [unless, of course, there has been a union of these natures, as was the case with Christ?] For if a hypostasis is an individual manifestation or example of a nature, it follows that the number of hypostases present in any given situation must at least equal the number of natures present. For each nature (to be present) must subsist in and be represented by at least one hypostasis. For a nature cannot subsist on its own and in the abstract, without at least one individual instance of that nature (or hypostasis.) [We could not, for example, say that "human nature" is present in a situation, when there is not a single "human person" (or hypostasis) present.]

Thus it is that those who profess that there is both a single hypostasis and a single nature in Christ—on account of the marvelous and unique union of Divinity and humanity which is present in Him—speak in a manner which is congruent with logic and reason, and consistent with the Truth. But those who insist that He is one hypostasis but two natures speak in a way which is both irreconcilable to reason and the meaning of words, and inconsistent with the Truth itself.

Chapter VIII

[As has been noted,] there are some who wish to say that there are two natures in Christ for the purpose (so they say) of avoiding any suggestion of "confusion" of His Divine and human nature. But if this is their fear, then they should also say that there are three natures in Christ—namely, the Divinity, the soul, and the body. For "human nature" is itself a union of a physical body and a rational soul. Yet we always speak of a human being as of one nature, and encounter no problematic confusion because of the union of body and soul which this implies and expresses.

But if Christ is a union of Divine nature and human nature, and human nature is itself a union of body and soul, those who refuse to admit that "oneness" is the necessary result of union are logically bound to say that Christ has three natures!

On the other hand, if we accept that human nature (composed of the union of body and soul) is, in fact, one, then why should we not say that the nature of Christ (in which there is a union of Divinity and humanity) is also one? Indeed, the union of Divinity and humanity in Christ was incomparably more perfect and complete than is the union of body and soul in an ordinary human being. If this latter union (which is merely natural and imperfect) gives rise to oneness, how much more should the former union (which is supernatural and perfect) result in oneness!

Later on in this work, we shall expound on the phrase "unconfused union."[9] But for the moment, let those who refuse to speak of "one nature" in Christ either say [as their thinking would seem to require] that He has "three natures" (that is, Divinity, body and soul); or else let them acknowledge that unity is the necessary result of union, and that, just as the union of body and soul in

---

9 See Chapter X

any human being results in one person, so the union of Divinity and humanity produces the one nature (both Divine and human) of Christ. By saying "two natures" rather than "three natures," there are bound [by the same principle of union] to say "one nature" rather than "two."

But what else do the proponents of the "two natures" terminology assert? Something quite foolish and insane. For they say something like the following: "There are not three natures in Christ, but two, and these two are the created and the uncreated natures. For the human soul and body are together the created nature, while the Divine nature is His uncreated nature. And so there are two natures in Christ—one which is created and the other uncreated—and not three [and not one]!"

But such an assertion reflects profound ignorance on how natures and substances are identified and distinguished from each other.[10] For if there was such a thing as a single generic "created nature" (meaning "a nature of created things") it would necessarily embrace and include every single thing in the whole created universe! For then the most splendid angel of heaven and a tiny gnat would both be said to be of the one nature, i.e., "created." But the condition of being created does not in any way describe or identify a nature or essence. For a nature is meaningfully identified on the basis of its substance and defining features, and the condition of having been created cannot actually serve as a description of a substance or nature at all.

And even if the "condition of having been created" is accepted as an attribute of an entity, this one attribute is clearly not sufficient to define or describe its nature. Otherwise, we would be bound to say that things which are evidently of entirely different natures [such as an angel and a gnat] are of one nature (of "having been created"). And that would clearly be absurd.

---

10 The text which follows in the remainder of this chapter is rather complex in the original, and difficult to render in comprehensible English. For this reason, it has been substantially paraphrased, while retaining carefully the substance of its argument.

Chapter VIII

And if we were asked if a horse and a man are of one and the same nature, we would not assert that they are, because they happen to have one or two attributes in common (such as the fact that they both walk, or both are white, [or are both created].) Neither would we say two things are of a different nature because they exhibit differences in a single attribute (unless it is attribute which is a defining quality, and constitutive of their nature). Such as in the case of a human beings, where one may be a Scythian or an Ethiopian, and one may have a long nose and another a flat nose, and where one may be a master and another a servant—yet they are all of the same human nature. For these particular properties and attributed are not what is constitutive and essential to human nature.

In a similar way, the condition of "having been created" is in no way constitutive of a nature, since it contains no meaningful description or identifying features of a substance or entity. It is therefore not plausible to speak of a "created nature," signifying a "nature of created things" in a general sense. Thus the assertion that Christ has both "the nature of having been created" and "the nature of not having been created" is neither logically tenable, nor even meaningful.

Chapter IX

It is to be noted that the words "divided" and "divisible" do not signify the same thing; nor do the words "undivided" and "indivisible" have the same meaning. For the term "divided" means that something has actually undergone a division; whereas "divisible" means that something could be divided, but has not yet been divided. Similarly, "undivided" means that something has not undergone a division, whereas "indivisible" indicates that something cannot be divided, or does not admit any possibility of being divided. The opposite of "divided" is "undivided," and the opposite of "divisible" is [obviously] "indivisible."

[It is all to be noted that all orthodox Christians] profess a belief that the unique and marvelous union of Divinity and humanity which took place through the Incarnation of Christ is indivisible. Now, if this union is indivisible, then the union (that is to say, the unity which results from the union) cannot be divided. And duality or "twoness" is nothing other than a division (as we have demonstrated in Chapter IV), for there cannot be twoness unless there is a separation or division between the elements which are numbered as two. But that which results from a union is not able to be two, or accurately to be described as being two—[for that would contradict the very meaning of "union," which is "making one."]

It was Christ who was born from the union of Divine and human natures. If this union was indivisible [as all profess and agree], it follows that it cannot admit division (which is the pre-condition and origin of twoness). Therefore it is impossible to assert that Christ has two natures, without undermining or denying the indivisibility of the union of Divinity and humanity which was achieved in the Incarnation.

Chapter X

This tenth [and final] chapter shall be dedicated to the refutation of the various objection to what we have advanced here which have been raised by our opponents. For I believe that it is evident to anyone that by successfully refuting the views and arguments of those who disagree with us, we thereby prove the truth of our own position.

[To commence our refutations of the various objections to the unity of Christ's nature, there are] those who say: "If Christ is of the same substance as God the Father in His Divinity, and of the same substance as us in His humanity, then there must be two natures in Christ, and not one. For if He is of the same substance with two different things (i.e., God and humanity) and these two things are not of the same substance as each other, then it follows that He has two different natures." In response to this, we point out that we do not hold that the nature of Christ to be simple, but rather to be composite. For if it were simple, it would be true that it could not simultaneously be of the same substance as two others things which are not of the same substance as each other. But the nature of Christ is the result of the union of Divinity and humanity, and therefore composite. He is nature is both Divine and human. In respect to the fact that His nature is Divine, Christ is of the same substance as God the Father; in respect to the fact that His nature is human, He is of the same substance as other human beings.

To illustrate this, the case of any human being may be considered. Human nature is itself composite, being a union of a physical body and an incorporeal soul. Therefore, we can say that a human being is of the same substance as physical objects, insofar as the composite nature of a human being includes a physical body. But we could equally say that a human being is the same substance as incorporeal or spiritual beings [such as angels or spirits], insofar as the composite nature of a human being includes an incorporeal soul. These two aspects of the single nature of human beings are referred to metaphorically by Paul as the "inner man" and the "outer man."[11] This does not, however, negate the essential unity of human nature.

We could likewise describe water is of the same substance as air, in respect to humidity [for air is often humid—that is to say, it has the aspect of water in a certain respect.] But we could also say that water is of the same substance as earth, in regard to the property of coldness [for both water and earth are typically exhibit the property of coldness.] Despite this, water does not possess two natures.

In a similar way, Christ is of the same substance as God the Father in respect to His Divinity, and of the same substance as other human beings in respect to His humanity. But this does not mean that He has two natures. For neither His Divinity or His humanity alone make up the whole nature of Christ. And this one nature is not, in its totality and uniqueness, identical with the nature of either God the Father or other human beings; despite the fact that, in its separated aspects, it is indeed of a common substance with each. We may divide His Divinity and humanity conceptually, to identify this likeness in substance with both God the Father and other human beings; but, in reality, He is one individual and one undivided and indivisible nature.

To take another consideration to demonstrate this point: through baptism, we all believe in one Lord Jesus Christ, and profess that "there is one God the Father, out of whom all things were created, and one Lord Jesus Christ, through whom all things were made."[12] Thus we very clearly do not believe that there are two Sons!

---

11 See 2 Corinthians 4:16
12 1 Corinthians 8:6.

Chapter X

And I am not here trying to refute the manifest error of the Nestorians, who absurdly claim that the Son proceeding from God is the Son of God by nature, yet the son proceeding from Mary is not the Son of God by nature, but only given this title by the indwelling of the Divinity and out of reverence and honor. Indeed, Nestorius himself realized this opinion was confounded by the words of the Holy Spirit [in Sacred Scripture], and so feebly tried to conceal his error by also asserting that these "two Sons" were also one Son "in honor and person."

[The next objection which we will refute is related to the observation we have just offered. For there are those who assert:] "If there is really one Son, our Lord Jesus Christ, how is it that we call Him both 'Son of God' (according to His Divinity), and 'Son of Man' (according to His humanity). For if He is Son of God in one sense, and Son of Man in another sense, then it seems as if He is in reality 'two Sons'—the Son of God, and the Son of Man. But if Christ is one Son, then there are two possibilities: either He is the Son of God only, or the Son of Man only. Otherwise, one seems bound to admit that Christ is two distinct Sons—the Son of God and the Son of Man."

[But this reasoning is faulty.] For if we recognize that Christ is the true and natural Son of God in His Divinity, and also the true Son of Man in His humanity (that is, "of the seed of David in His flesh"[13]) Christ is nevertheless perfectly one, though His nature proceeds both from Divinity and from humanity. In the first respect He is truly the Son of God, and of one substance with God the Father. In the second respect He is truly the Son of Man, and of one substance with other human beings. Now, if this really means that He has two natures, the same logic would equally imply that there are two Sons, because He is the Son both of God and of Man. But if there are not two Sons (because of the miraculous union which has taken place), then neither

---

13 Romans 1:3

will there be two natures (again, because of the same mystical union).

There are also those who say: "If the natures of Christ remain unconfused after the union, and if neither His Divine nature nor His human nature have undergone any mutation or variation, how can you say that they are now one nature instead of two? For if the two natures both remained completely and perfectly unchanged [after the Incarnation], then surely they must still be two natures, just as they were before!" But we are able to refute this specious argument with the following reply: "If both of the natures (that is, Divine and human) were each one beforehand, and unity was an essential feature of these natures, then, if they truly remain unchanged, they necessarily will still be a unity after the Incarnation." For if there was duality in the nature of Christ, there must be division, which is in contradiction to union and unity.

Those who maintain that such a union cannot occur without a confusion or impairment of the elements of the union are speaking falsely. Indeed, we can offer a multitude of examples from nature of union without confusion, to refute this argument. Firstly, human beings are a union of a physical body and a rational and incorporeal soul. Yet the essential unity of the human being is acknowledged, and there never arises any problematic confusion because of this union. If anyone should [foolishly] assert that a human being has two natures, we would refute him with the same arguments we have advanced regarding Christ—[namely, that union, by definition, results in a unity.] Admittedly, there are those who describe the rational soul as being the principal part of the human being, who is defined as a "rational animal"; nevertheless, this does not undermine the fact that human nature is essentially united. This example is, as we have mentioned, well-known to everyone.

Another example is air which is illuminated by light shining through it. Now, clearly such illuminated air is the result of the union of air and light. The nature of the air and light are not confused, but they are united in such a manner that no separation of the two can be perceived or detected. If they are spoken of separately, this division is only conceptual and not present or visible in reality.

The same could also be said of water which is illuminated by light shining through it, or any other substance which exhibits the same phenomenon. For glass and transparent gemstones also admit the element of light into themselves. But when light illuminates such a substance [whether air, water, glass, or stone], the natures, though truly united in each case, are by no means confused. For when light shines through air, there is no portion of that air which is separable from the light; nor is there any light which is separable from the air. Therefore, no separation is detectable. For these two natures—air and light—have produced a single united nature, namely, that of illuminated air.

The light which shines in illuminated air is thus in a state of true union with that air. Indeed, light proceeding from the sun never exists in a state of separation from some other nature, for it bestows its radiance upon all things under the heavens, and cannot proceed from the sun without passing through or shining upon some other substance or body.

But [to return to the example of illuminated air], neither the light nor the air (though indivisibly united) suffers any impairment or confusion in their respective natures. For the light retains its essential brightness, and the air retains all the properties which are constitutive of the nature of air. If the light passes out of the air, it still remains light (just as it was before). And if the light ceases to shine upon the air, the air retains the nature of air without any impairment.

But those things which are united in such a way that their nature is altered or varied or confused can never be restored to their original nature, if a division was undertaken. For the essential nature which they had beforehand has been destroyed or impaired. A case of this would be the mixture of wine and honey, or honey in water. [In neither case, can the original elements be satisfactorily restored to what they were before the union.] Another such case is the human body. After death, it is sometimes said to decay and "return to the elements." But those who are knowledgeable about such matters will realize that a decomposed organic body does not, in fact, return to the same elements from which it was constituted, but quite different ones. [Thus a human body, composed from the various elements of food and drink which nourish it, does not return to these when it decays, but rather to dust, earth, and putridity.]

But it is quite different in the case of the union of air and light, in which the natures remained unconfused and suffer no loss of their proper character. This may be compared to a person receiving instruction and gaining understanding of some field of knowledge. Though he has become united with the new knowledge he has come to acquire, his nature does certainly not cease to be that of a human being. And air, even when illuminated by its union with light, remains air [while the light remains light. But the union of the two is perfect and complete.]

It behooves us to consider the union of Divine and human natures which occurred in the Incarnation in a similar way. For God the Word has attained humanity through this Incarnation, but His Divinity remains undiminished and unaltered. The human nature of Christ, too, remains essentially and completely human, and has in no way been negated or altered. The examples from the natural world of unconfused union which we have provided are sufficient to demonstrate that two natures may be truly united, and yet the essential character of the united natures is not thereby destroyed, or altered in such a way that it loses its essential and defining characteristics. These examples, which are clear and easily understood, demonstrate that a union of natures does not necessarily imply a confusion of their properties, or a destruction of their essential characteristics.

Chapter X

So much for examples! Now, it is clear that a destruction or confusion of natures is implied and necessitated only when the natures which are united are somehow contradictory to each other. Thus, for example, if heat is mixed with coldness, or black is mixed with white, the essential properties of the natures involved will be lost or negated [since they are mutually contradictory.]

But this happens only when the characteristics concerned pertain to the same property or parameter. For heat and coldness are contradictory with respect to the same property—namely, temperature. And whiteness and blackness are contradictory in respect to the same property—namely, color. Thus, they cannot co-exist with negating the essential nature of each. But natures which are not contradictory with respect to the same property can readily be united without any negation of the essential characteristics of the natures concerned. Thus, for example, in an apple, sweetness of flavor is combined with roundness of shape. But there is no contradiction here, or negation of either the properties of sweetness or of roundness. For both of these pertain to predicates or values which are independent of each other.[14]

But just as soul and body [which are united in each human being] are not contrary or mutually incompatible properties, so neither are Divinity and humanity [which were united in Christ] contradictory. In the case of soul and body, they cannot be thought of contradictory, since one is incorporeal and other is corporeal; therefore, there are of an entirely different genus and order. Now, if this is the case, how much more is it true of Divinity and humanity! [For Divinity differs from humanity as much as the soul differs from the body—indeed, much more so, since one is transcendent, infinite and eternal, and the other is circumscribed and finite.]

Thus those who would deny the union of Divinity and humanity in Christ because the imagined fear of some possible "confusion"

---

14 The original text has been abridged slightly here, for the sake of clarity and readability. The point being made is relatively simple and is sufficiently demonstrated in the explanation given above.

fall into madness and folly! And they assert two contradictory and irreconcilable opinions—that Christ is one hypostasis, but two natures. We have already shown [in Chapter VII] that this is logically impossible and absurd.

Next, we will consider the objection of those who boldly dare to ask: "If Christ is only one nature, then which of His two natures—Divine or human—has been destroyed?" For this absurd question is assuming that the single nature of Christ is simple, and not composite. If we, who assert the unity of the nature of Christ, were saying that it was a simple nature [either Divine or human, but not both], this question might be justified. But if it is a composite nature (resulting from the unconfused union of Divinity and humanity) then neither nature has been "destroyed." For if either of the natures had, in fact, been destroyed, the resulting nature would not be composite at all, but simple.

But there are those who dare to decry our use of the term "composite" for the nature of Christ, even though such terminology is employed by countless doctors of the Church. They say: "If the nature of the Divinity is simple and not composite, and the nature of Christ is (as you assert) composite from the union of Divinity and humanity, then the original, simple nature of God has been transformed into a composite nature, and therefore lost its essential simplicity." Alas, this objection exhibits immense ignorance of philosophy and dullness of mind! For the natures which, through union, produce a composite nature do not, in themselves, thereby become composite.

To refer again to the example of a human being, the rational soul and the physical body are each simple (or at least simple, in comparison with the composite nature of a complete human being). Now, these do not cease, in themselves, to be simple because of the fact that they have undergone a union. To give a further example, if we consider a white stone, it has united the nature of a stone and the nature of whiteness. But whiteness does not lose its essential simplicity, even in the context of this union. For if whiteness thereby became composite, what are the elements which have been combined to produce this composite state? And if, extrapolating the erroneous premise that the elements in a composite necessarily also become composite themselves. And then these elements (which are now supposedly composite) would have to be composed of other elements, which, in turn, would also be composite. And this process would continue ad infinitum!

If we consider an even more irrefutable example—the number four is composed of four units, or four "ones." Now, each of these unities remains simple; they do not each become fours!

But if anything is formed from the union of different elements or natures (i.e., it is composed of these different elements) then, by definition, it is a composite.

In the case of Christ, the spiritual character, immortality and eternity of the Divinity are preserved and undiminished in the composite nature of Christ, although they were united to a human body which was physical and subject to suffering. But the simplicity and immortality of Divinity are in no sense negated by this union.

Perhaps some people may object to the idea of a union of natures in Christ in the following terms: "If Christ is a composite nature, formed from the union of Divinity and humanity, it follows that each of these participants in the union was, in some sense, incomplete. For the part is always less than the whole. [And if one asserts that the Divinity is only a 'part' of this union, its absolutely perfection, completion and supremacy are being denied.]"

This objection, however, is specious and false. For anything is described as a "part" only insofar as it contributes to some particular whole. In this sense, becoming a part of something does not imply any imperfection in the thing itself. To give a commonplace example, a rudder is a part of a ship, and a wheel is a part of a chariot. But this does not mean that somehow either the rudder or the wheel was imperfect in themselves. They may seem to be "incomplete" only if we consider them in respect to the totality of either the ship or the chariot. But if we consider them in themselves, they are perfect and complete.

A further illustration may be drawn from electrum [which is an alloy made from gold and silver.] Now, someone might foolishly say: "Since gold is only a part of electrum, it follows that gold must be less perfect and inferior in value to electrum, which is the whole." It may seem less perfect or complete, only if we try to consider the gold as electrum! But if we consider it in itself, it is certainly not imperfect or incomplete; nor, indeed, is it of lesser value than the electrum. And there are innumerable other instances and examples which could be cited.

It is fitting that we should consider the case of Our Lord Jesus Christ in this way. Though Divinity is a part of His composite nature, it does not follow (because it is a part of this nature) that it is somehow incomplete or imperfect in itself. Indeed, the Divine nature is utterly perfect in every respect, and transcends comparison with everything which exists! And this Divinity, as the ultimate perfection, cannot be considered inferior to anything [even the nature of Christ, although this Divinity is but one element in the union which produced His unique nature.]

[To return to the essence of these objections,] what is there which prevents us from describing the fruit of the union of several elements as being "one" instead of "several"? [To give a simple and clear example of this,] I may correctly say: "A triangle is formed from three straight lines. Yet these form a single triangle, which is one. Thus these three straight lines [united to form a triangle] are one and not many." To provide another example. The properties or natures of heat, lightness and dryness are each to be found in fire. But fire has but one nature. Therefore, these three—heat, lightness and dryness—form the one nature of fire.

Chapter X

I think it is clear to all those whose minds are open to perceiving the logic of the matter that the conclusion has now been made sufficiently evident. Hence it is not necessary for any further objections to be enumerated and refuted. But we will present a final, simple statement of the case: If a house consists of stones, walls and planks of timber, the form of the house is still one, and this one house includes stones, walls and timber. If three straight lines together form a single triangle, the resultant form is one triangle, which includes three straight lines. And the same may be said of fire and many other examples—indeed, of each and every composite nature.

Similarly, although the nature of the Incarnate Christ proceeds from the union of two natures—Divinity and humanity—it is not necessary, on account of this, to say that Christ Himself has two natures. For, [through the miraculous union which occurred in His Incarnation,] these two natures have become truly and indivisibly one. We need not (and shall not) be led, by our profession of the oneness of Christ, to deny or compromise either of the two elements which constitute His nature (i.e., His Divinity and his humanity). Neither, in professing the truth of both the Divinity and the humanity of Christ, need we be led to deny His perfect unity.

It makes no difference to our argument whether someone prefers to call this essential unity of Christ "one nature" or "one hypostasis" or simply "one Christ." For all of these expressions imply the others. For if Christ is one, His nature and His hypostasis are necessarily one as well. If the unity of Christ is not to be divided, He must be one nature and one hypostasis. For how can what is numbered as being two be, in reality, one? [And how can what is in reality one, be correctly numbered as two?] That the same reality should simultaneously be both one and two is an impossibility. How could two separate natures be one hypostasis? And how could an individual being of one particular and unique nature be anything other than a single hypostasis?

Epilogue

We have, in this short work, set forth our argument and demonstrations as well as our modest abilities permit. Now we exhort all those who read this treatise that, without prejudice and without any human bias, they objectively evaluate the truth and soundness of what we have advanced. If they discover that what we have said is sound and logical, let them put aside all envy, and accept it out of pure love of the truth, as if it were their very own dear child. For (I believe) whatever of the truth is discovered or demonstrated serves the common benefit of all humanity, regardless of who it is who discovers it.

But if anyone finds that our judgments or reasoning is unsound or faulty, we can only humbly implore their forgiveness. But may they also give healing along with forgiveness, by advancing their own clear rebuttals and refutations of our errors. For it is a benefit to each human being to be corrected in their errors and so to be liberated from ignorance; and whoever does this for another ought to be regarded as their truest benefactor and friend.

Here concludes the ten chapters of the work entitled 'The Arbiter' [or 'The Wise Judge.']

Introduction Bibliography

The Biblical Repository. Flagg & Gould, 1834. https://books.google.com.au/books?id=7oAXAAAAYAAJ.

Botros, A., and Saint George Coptic Orthodox Church. The Coptic Liturgy of Saint Basil with Raising of Incense. Saint George Coptic Orthodox Church, 1999. https://books.google.com.au/books?id=0YUbAAAACAAJ.

Church, Coptic, St. Bakhomious St. Mary, and St. Shenouda Coptic Orthodox Church. Midnight Praises. St Mary, St Bakhomios & St Shenouda Coptic Orthodox Church, 2007. https://books.google.com.au/books?id=fGVXNQAACAAJ.

Current, J.D. Physics Related to Anesthesia. PediaPress GmbH, 2010. https://books.google.com.au/books?id=RgcpOQ444vgC.

Davidson, Herbert A. "John Philoponus as a Source of Medieval Islamic and Jewish Proofs of Creation." Journal of the American Oriental Society 89, no. 2 (1969): 357-91. https://doi.org/10.2307/596519. http://www.jstor.org/stable/596519.

Kelly, T. The a to Z of People of Faith and Science: Short Biographies. ATF Press, 2018. https://books.google.com.au/books?id=Le-YDwAAQBAJ.

Lang, P. Science: Antiquity and Its Legacy. Bloomsbury Publishing, 2015. https://books.google.com.au/books?id=dbeKDwAAQBAJ.

Lang, U.M. John Philoponus and the Controversies over Chalcedon in the Sixth Century: A Study and Translation of the Arbiter. Peeters, 2001. https://books.google.com.au/books?id=342CNwaH8vsC.

McKenna, J.E. The Setting in Life for the Arbiter of John Philoponos, 6th Century Alexandrian Scientist. Wipf and Stock Publishers, 1997. https://books.google.com.au/books?id=WWVKAwAAQBAJ.

McKenna, John. The Concept of Nature in the Thought of John Philoponus and Other Essays. Grace Communion International, 2015.

Philoponus, J., and M.J. Share. Against Proclus on the Eternity of the World 1-5. Duckworth, 2004. https://books.google.com.au/books?id=iuvWAAAAMAAJ.

Sorabji, R. Philoponus and the Rejection of Aristotelian Science. Institute of Classical Studies, School of Advanced Study, University of London, 2010. https://books.google.com.au/books?id=EW5CAQAAIAAJ.

Torrance, A., and S. Paschalidis. Personhood in the Byzantine Christian Tradition: Early, Medieval, and Modern Perspectives. Taylor & Francis, 2018. https://books.google.com.au/books?id=oKVYDwAAQBAJ.

Torrance, T.F. Theological and Natural Science. Wipf & Stock Publishers, 2005. https://books.google.com.au/books?id=PbJKAwAAQBAJ.

Zachhuber, J. The Rise of Christian Theology and the End of Ancient Metaphysics: Patristic Philosophy from the Cappadocian Fathers to John of Damascus. Oxford University Press, 2020. https://books.google.com.au/books?id=PnbnDwAAQBAJ.

www.ingramcontent.com/pod-product-compliance
Lightning Source LLC
Chambersburg PA
CBHW031204160426
43193CB00008B/492